From Pen To Paper

A Lifetime Of Sentences
Waiting To Be Heard

Marvin Louis Beauchamp

From Pen To Paper
A Lifetime Of Sentences Waiting To Be Heard
Author: Marvin Louis Beauchamp

ISBN 13: 978-1-940961-54-5
ISBN 10: 1940961-54-8

First Printing 2018

Printed in the United States of America

To order additional copies, please visit www.RIVObooks.com

We'd love to hear from you regarding your support for Mr. Beauchamp. Please email us at: order@RIVOinc.com and we will forward your kind words of support and encouragement.

Dedication

I dedicate this book to:
My Mother (Grandma Cill)
My Aunt Jackie, My Aunt "Reese"
My Brother ST. (Dad),
My Star, My Beautiful Andrain,
My Boys: Jordan, Jah'vaughn, Jaitin & Jayvion,
My Girls: Jazlyn, Abrina, Ava & Avrie.

"You Can Do Whatever You Put Your Mind To Because GOD Chose You Too!"

In Loving Memory Of

Sherida Davis
Rosa Johnson & Kelly Swetow

Sherida was my friend who was killed in a
murder-suicide by her husband
(who was a Milwaukee Police Officer) in 2016.

Rosa was a friend of my Mother who started
this journey with me, being very supportive.

Kelly is my Nephew's Mother, who committed
suicide last month in 2018.

They all would have been very proud of me!

Inside are the raw expressed emotions from the psyche of a man searching for himself.

We all experience these feelings, but not all of us can decipher their many differences enough to capture them and explore their true meaning.

The thoughts and feelings in this book have been made tangible, so that you can feel exactly what the author was experiencing while writing.

These writings are being shared with the hope of helping you, the reader, clarify some of your past, present and future feelings.

The mirror only reflects what everyone else can see.

♥'AW'♥

    THERE'S A YOUNG LADY THAT I KNOW WHO MAKES ME THINK TWICE WHEN EVER I AM READY TO GIVE UP ON MYSELF AND STOP BEING PERSISTENT.

    HER PRESENCE HASN'T GRACED THIS EARTH FOR VERY LONG, NOR HAVE I EVER MET HER IN PERSON, BUT WE ARE AWARE OF EACH OTHERS' EXISTENCE.

    THE ARRIVAL OF HER LIFE WAS EXTREMELY EARLY, SO MUCH SO, DOCTORS GAVE HER A 50% CHANCE OF SURVIVAL.

    SHE SURVIVED! PROVING THAT, GOD AND ONLY GOD DECIDES.

    THE SURVIVAL SHE WAS BLESSED WITH GIVES ME THE STRENGTH NEEDED TO FIGHT FOR MYSELF.

    HER BATTLE FOR LIFE, CAUSED THE LEVEL OF FIGHT IN MY LIFE TO BECOME HIGHER

    BECAUSE HER LIFE WAS MY VERY FIRST PRAYER, WITHOUT SELFISH DESIRE.

    RIGHT NOW SHE'S TOO YOUNG, BUT ONE DAY SHE WILL UNDERSTAND, HOW HER LIFE WAS A TESTAMENT TO A GROWN MAN, ABOUT THE AWESOME, UNDENIABLE, POWERFUL, STRENGTH OF GOD'S HAND. . . . (B).

"FROM PEN TO PAPER"

      AS I WIELD MY WEAPON OF CHOICE,
A WAY, I MUST FIND TO TRANSCRIBE THE
VOICE INSIDE MY MIND, THAT NEVER QUITS
SPEAKING.
      INSIDE THE BATTLE OF MY MIND
WHATS SPILLED IS NOT BLOOD, IT IS INK
THAT IS LEAKING.
      FROM THE PEN TO THE PAPER
IS THE ONLY WAY I ACTUALLY RECOGNIZE
WHAT I AM THINKING.
      DRAFTING A BLUEPRINT FROM THE
MEASUREMENTS OF FEELINGS IVE BEEN
TAUGHT TO SURPRESS.
      THOUGHTS OOZE FROM MY PENS TIP
REVEALING TRUTHS THAT VERBALLY I
CANNOT EXPRESS.
      THE TIGHTER I SQUEEZE THE PEN
THE MORE INK DRIPS ON THE PAPER.
      WHAT I CANT SAY WITH MY LIPS IS
TURNED INTO SCRIPT, TRANSFORMING MY
PEN INTO MY UNCONSCIOUS DICTATOR.
      DUE TO THERE BEING NO LANGUAGE
TO DESCRIBE THIS ANGUISH. I AM FORCED
TO LISTEN TO MY MINDS CONVERSATION, THAT
OF, I AM NOT A PART.

IF I TRY TO TUNE IT OUT
I BECOME TRAPPED INTO LISTENING
TO MY HEART.
    THAT IS A CONVERSATION THAT'LL
MAKE THE STRONGEST MAN DELIRIOUS.
    NO ONE TAKES ME SERIOUS!
    I'M NOT SURE AS TO WHY,
THE ONLY TIME ANYONE UNDERSTANDS
ME IS WHEN MY PENS' INK RUNS DRY.
    OFCOURSE, REMAINING SILENT
WOULD BE MUCH SAFER, BUT I WOULD
RATHER SCREAM LOUDLY FROM THE
PEN TO THE PAPER.

"I AM"

I AM NOT MY THOUGHTS

I AM WHO RECOGNIZES MY THOUGHTS
THEREFORE I AM NOT WHO I AM

I AM LOOKING FROM THE OUTSIDE
YET I AM INSIDE AT THE SAME TIME.

I AM NOT WHO I AM
AT LEAST I AM NOT IN MY MIND.

I AM MY THOUGHTS
ONLY I KNOW WHAT I AM THINKING

IF INDEED I AM MY THOUGHTS
HOW CAN I RECOGNIZE WHAT
I AM THINKING?

"LIFE THE BOOK"

Everything that happens in life has happend before any time ever passed.

The Book of Life has long before been written, yet you dont know how your character plays out or if it will even last.

Each Chapter of Existence will have its surprises, before each chapter ends, there will be a twist.

You find yourself trying to go back even though its too late to re-read things that you missed

You'll never be able to predict the outcome this book was written by the author of all authors, the best author that there will ever be.

In order to find out what happens in the end, you'll just have to wait and see.

This is the longest book in history, or at least, the longest book that you will ever know.

Theres supposedly a part two but those who have read it arent around, so they cant show us its contents, or give us a hint to what happens in the end.

WONDERING WHERE THE FIRST
BOOK STOPS. AND WHERE THE SECOND ONE BEGINS.
MAYBE THIS IS THE SECOND BOOK
AND WHEN IT ENDS, IT MOVES RIGHT INTO PART
THREE.

IN ORDER TO FIND OUT WHAT HAPPENS
IN THE END, YOU'LL JUST HAVE TO WAIT
AND SEE. ⓑ.

"Concrete Garden"

Have you ever visited a concrete garden?

Did you stop to smell a concrete rose?

If so, was the smell unfamiliar to your nose.

A new one grows daily and you had no clue that they even existed.

If it weren't for me being an horticulturist, you probably would have missed it.

These gardens are usually found in dismal places, deeply rooted in fields of sorrow and hurt.

All it takes is a little fear an instantly a new one appears, ready to stand proud, its only nourishment are tears

Once they are fully grown they will never wither, just harden.

By the way, roses aren't the only thing that grows in a concrete garden

"SEEKING"

HAPPINESS IS WHAT'S SOUGHT AFTER.
EMPTINESS IS WHATS USUALLY FOUND.
ONLY SILENCE TO BE HEARD
ONLY DARKNESS AROUND.
THROUGH THE SILENCE
SCREAMS OF AGONY BEING HEARD COMING
FROM A UNKNOWN SOURCE.
TRYING TO IGNORE THEM
BUT YOU CAN RECOGNIZE THE VOICE.
SEARCHING FOR THE SCREAMS
AFRAID OF WHOM YOU MAY FIND.
HOPING THAT YOU ARE DREAMING
AND THIS IS ALL IN YOUR MIND.
AS YOU GET CLOSER
YOU NOTICE THE SCREAMS HAVE TURNED
INTO LAUGHTER.
I GUESS THE IDEA IS PRETTY
FUNNY, YOU KNOW, THE THOUGHT OR
HAPPINESS BEING SOUGHT AFTER . . .

"LIFE THE SPORT"

THERE'S NOTHING TO ENSURE YOUR
SAFETY, NO PROTECTIVE GEAR OF ANY KIND.
NO COOPERATION AT ALL, FROM ANYONE
OPPOSING PLAYERS IS ALL YOU'LL FIND.
THERE'S NO REFEREE, WHISTLE BLOWN,
OR FLAG THROWN WHEN YOU'VE BEEN WRONGED.
NO PAUSE IN EVENTS HALFWAY THROUGH
NO HALFTIME SHOW OR PEOPLE SINGING SONGS.
THERE'S NO FAMOUS COMENTATORS
TO RECAP THE GAME.
NO REPLAY CAMERA
TO RESHOW THE MISTAKES YOU MADE.
THERE'S NO QUARTERS
HALFS, SETS, OR INNINGS.
NO CROWD TO CHEER YOU ON
ONLY YOU CARE IF YOU ARE WINNING.
THERE'S NO ENDORSEMENTS
COMMERCIALS, OR JERSEYS THAT DISPLAY YOUR NAME
YOU ARE A STARTING PLAYER AND YOU ARE
FORCED TO PLAY THIS GAME.
FORCED TO PLAY THIS GAME?
YES, YOU ARE UNABLE TO ABORT.
WHAT'S THE NAME OF THIS COMPETITION
I CALL IT LIFE THE SPORT. Ⓑ;

"Endangered Species"

I AM A RARE SPECIES THAT USED TO ROAM FREELY IN MY NATURAL HABITAT. THERE WERE AN ABUNDANCE OF MY KIND AT ONE POINT AND TIME. UNTIL ONE DAY WE WERE APPROVED AS FAIR GAME FOR HUNTING. HUNTERS KILL US OFF DAILY WITH NO REMORSE. THE ONES THAT ARENT KILLED OFF ARE TRAPPED AND SHIPPED TO VARIOUS ZOOS. THESE ZOOS PROVIDE AN ABUNDANCE OF JOBS, THERE HAS TO BE SOMEONE TO FEED US AND KEEP US ALIVE. IF THEY DIDNT, THEIR ZOOS WOULDN'T THRIVE, WHICH WOULD BE DETRIMENTAL TO CONTROL US BY KEEPING OUR POPULATION DOWN. DON'T GET ME WRONG, THEY ARE NOT THE ONLY PREDATORS WHO SEEK AND DESTROY MY KIND, MY VERY OWN SPECIES IS THE NUMBER ONE POACHER OF THEM ALL. THE OPPORTUNITIES NEEDED TO SOLIDIFY SURVIVAL ARE PROVIDED IN SUCH SHORT SUPPLY THAT WE FIGHT AND KILL ONE ANOTHER OVER WHAT IS MADE AVAILABLE TO US. THIS TOO IS PART OF THE ZOOKEEPERS PLAN, KILL US OFF BUT LET THE BLOOD STAIN OUR OWN HANDS. ONE DAY SOON MY SPECIES WILL HAVE TO LEARN HOW TO CHANNEL ALL OF THEIR NEGATIVE ENERGY AND ANGER INTO POSITIVE THINGS, SUCH AS, WAYS TO KEEP US OFF OF

THE LIST OF SPECIES THAT ARE ENDANGERED.

UNFORTUNATELY; RIGHT NOW, THE BLIND IS LEADING THE BLIND, WITH HATE, HAND IN HAND.

ONE DAY SOON, LOVE FOR ONE ANOTHER, IS GOING TO HAVE TO BE FOR WHICH WE STAND.

THAT IS THE ONLY WAY WE WILL EVER BE SUCCESSFUL IN SAVING MY SPECIES ...

... THE BLACKMAN!

"INFINITY"

Tomorrow should be called infinity.
No matter what it will always come.
It may not come for many
But it will come for some.
Yesterday should be calle infinity
It will always be the past.
No matter how far away Tomorrow is
Today will never last.
Today could never be infinite
It is always over too soon.
Knowing that tomorrow is approaching
It leaves to make room.
Today leaves, Tomorrow comes
Adding to yesterdays count.
Its impossible to keep track
Because infinity is the amount.

"CHEER"

Smile for me today
Smile for you tomorrow
Smiling helps to ease the pain of
yesterday's sorrow.
Laugh for me now
Laugh for you later
Then laugh some more when you
are done.
Laugh before your day has ended
and laugh before it has begun.
Smiling and laughing should flow
freely, they go hand in hand.
It takes more energy
to frown and cry
I prefer laughing and smiling
Try it for yourself and you'll see
why. Ⓑ

"ADDICTION"

I THINK I AM AN ADDICT
I FIND MYSELF FIENDING FOR YOUR LOVE
CAN'T LIVE WITHOUT YOU IN MY LIFE, CRAVING
FOR YOUR VERY TOUCH.

    IVE GOT TO BE AN ADDICT
JUST LIKE A DRUG ALL IT TOOK, WAS ONE
DOSE OF YOUR LOVE AND IMMEDIATELY I
WAS HOOKED.

    I JUST MIGHT BE AN ADDICT
WITHOUT YOUR LOVE I'm SICK, IN DESPERATE
NEED OF AFFECTION AND YOUR PRESENCE I
NEED A FIX.

    I MUST BE AN ADDICT,
INTOXICATION LEVELS IN MY BLOOD ARE
OVER THE LIMIT
ITS BEEN THAT WAY FOR AWHILE
EVEN THOUGH MY LIFE
YOU HAVENT BEEN IN IT.

    LIKE AN ADDICT I WAS IN DENIAL
I THOUGHT I COULD KICK MY HABIT
BECAUSE I HAD YOUR LOVE SHOOK FOR
AWHILE.

    IVE CHECKED MYSELF INTO REHAB
NUMEROUS AMOUNTS OF TIMES, THINKING THAT

IT WOULD HELP CURE ME, AND GET
YOU OUTTA MY MIND.
    I FIND MYSELF DESIRING YOU
AT THE MERE THOUGHT OF YOUR BEAUTIFUL
FACE
    REALIZING I DONT WANT OR NEED
ANY HELP, BECAUSE YOU I COULD NEVER
REPLACE.
    SO ONCE AN ADDICT ALWAYS AN ADDICT
IS ALL I CAN REALLY SAY
    YOUR POWERFUL LOVE SATURATED
MY HEART, AND THE HIGH YOU GIVE
    I NEVER WANT IT TO GO AWAY . . .

"Beauty"

Beautiful you are
Beautiful indeed.
    Your beauty is so deep
It's all the beauty that I need.
    Beautiful you are
As a life partener, lover, and a friend.
    Beautiful you are
Out side, as well as in.
    Your beauty is like a priceless painting
on display for the entire world to see.
    If beauty is in the eyes of the
beholder, then allow me to be the one
to hold you, because you are beautiful
to me.

"TEARS"

SOMETIMES I FEEL LIKE CRYING
I CANT, SO WHEN IT RAINS I ALLOW THE
SKY TO SHED MY TEARS.

AS I SLUMBER, IM AFRAID OF WHAT
TOMORROW MAY BRING.

I KNOW I MUST OVERCOME MY
FEARS.

STUCK IN LIFE'S QUICKSAND, IF I MOVE TOO
QUICKLY ILL SINK DEEP.

HAPPINESS STILL LINGERS IN THE AIR,
MEMORIES OF GOODTIMES I MUST KEEP.

FIRST ONE CHOSEN TO PLAY, ONLY TO FIND
OUT IN THE END, THIS IS NO GAME.

THOUGHTS BUZZING AROUND IN MY HEAD,
AS IF THERE IS AN APIARY IN MY BRAIN.

AS I FILL ANOTHER BOTTLE WITH PAIN,
STORAGE SPACE IS BECOMING SNY.

ONE DAY SOON THERE WILL BE NO MORE
SPACE TO STORE BOTTLES, SO I GUESS I WILL HAVE
TO CRY

WHEN THE TEARS DO FINALLY COME, THEY
WILL BE TEARS OF JOY

BECAUSE ALL THE PAIN COLLECTED IN THESE
BOTTLES, I WILL NO LONGER HAVE TO STORE...

"WILL"

I CAN SEE THE EYES OF DOUBT
WANTING SEE FAILURE, ALONG WITH THE FACES
OF SKEPTICISM WATCHING.
F.Y.I.
FAILURE IS NOT AN OPTION
THE TAPE **WILL** BE CUT
NEW GROUND **WILL** BE BROKEN
ALL IN DUE TIME
THE MIND MUST BE KEPT OPEN
DREAMS **WILL** COME TRUE
THIS IS NO LONGER ABOUT HOPING AND WISHING
THE ORDER HAS BEEN GIVEN,
AND GRANTED, **WILL** BE A COMPLETED MISSION
THE OBJECTIVE IS VICTORY
THAT IS WHAT **WILL** BE GIVEN, BUT NOT
WITHOUT STRUGGLE AND PAIN.
THE WEATHER **WILL** NOT ALWAYS BE
SUNNY AND FAIR, THERE **WILL** BE NUMEROUS
PARADES RUINED BY RAIN
THE SKIES **WILL** SOON BECOME CLEAR
AND THE NUMBER ONE DRYING FORCE WILL
BE POWER OVER DEFEAT.

I CAN ASSURE YOU IN THE END THE EYES OF DOUBT AND THE EYES OF VICTORY WILL DEFINITELY MEET.

(D).

"Rich"

I AM PROOF THAT YOU CAN BE RICH
WITHOUT HAVING A DIME.

I AM RICH WITH THE TREASURE OF
KNOWLEDGE, STORED IN THE VAULTS OF MY
MIND.

I AM RICH WITH THE SPIRIT OF GOD
THAT KEEPS ME HUMBLE AND PURE.

I AM RICH WITH PATIENCE
THE HELPS ME ENDURE.

I AM RICH WITH AN ABUNDANCE OF LOVE
THAT MY HEART KEEPS UNDER LOCK AND KEY

I AM RICH WITH OPTIMISM
A BRIGHT FUTURE IS EASY TO SEE.

YOU TOO CAN BE RICH
THESE RICHES AREN'T THAT HARD TO FIND.

LOOK AT ME, I'M A PERFECT EXAMPLE
OF BEING RICH WITHOUT HAVING A DIME.

"A MAN?"

A MAN CONSISTS OF MORE THAN BEING A MALE
A MAN IS ABLE TO ADMIT WHEN HE HAS FAILED.
A MAN NEVER MAKES EXCUSES, OR FROM HIS
PROBLEMS DOES HE RUN.
A MAN MAKES SURE HE IS ALWAYS A FATHER
TO HIS SON; OR DAUGHTER, WHATEVER HIS
CHILDS GENDER MAY BE, FOR HIS ACTIONS
A MAN ALWAYS TAKES RESPONSIBILITY.
A MAN KNOWS HOW TO SWALLOW HIS PRIDE,
AND WHEN HE IS UNSURE, ALLOWS SOMEONE
ELSE TO BE HIS GUIDE.
A MAN KNOWS WHEN TO ASK FOR HELP OR DIRECTIONS
A MAN REALIZES THAT SOMETIMES THE PROTECTOR
NEEDS PROTECTION
A MAN IS NOT JUST REACHING A CERTAIN AGE.
A MAN IS NOT ASHAMED OF BEING AFRAID, SCARED,
OR NOT BEING PREPARED.
A MAN IS NOT MEASURED BY HIS FINANCIAL STATUS
OR PHYSICAL STRENGTH.
A MAN WORKS HARD FOR WHAT HE WANTS AND WITH
WHAT HE HAS HE IS CONTENT BECAUSE A MAN
KNOWS THAT THE GRASS ISN'T ALWAYS GREENER
ON THE OTHER SIDE OF THE FENCE
A MAN KNOWS HOW TO GIVE AS WELL AS

ACCEPT LOVE.
A MAN FEARS NO MAN BUT THE MAN
UP ABOVE.
ARE YOU A MAN!

("A MAN?2")

A MAN BEFORE LEANING ON SOMEONE ELSE
KNOWS HOW TO STAND ON HIS OWN TWO FEET.
A MAN IS HIS OWN MAN NO MATTER WHAT
ANY OTHER MAN DOES, SAYS, OR THINKS.
A MAN CONSISTS OF MORE THAN MALE
GENITALIA BELOW THE WAIST.
A MAN HAS HIS PRIORITIES IN ORDER AND
IF NOT HE WORKS TOWARDS MAKING THAT TRUE.
A MAN WHEN FACED WITH A PROBLEM WILL ASK
FOR HELP WHEN HE DOESNT KNOW WHAT TO DO.
A MAN IS ALWAYS PUNCTUAL, HE IS NEVER
LATE.
A MAN IS NOT IMPATIENT, HE KNOWS HOW TO
WAIT.
A MAN KNOWS HOW TO GIVE AS WELL AS
ACCEPT APOLOGIES WHEN THEY ARE GIVEN.
A MAN IS ALWAYS A GENTLEMAN WHEN IN
THE PRESENCE OF WOMEN
A MAN AVOIDS CONFLICT AT ALL COST.
A MAN CAN ACCEPT DEFEAT, HE CAN REALIZE
WHEN HE HAS LOST.
A MAN DOESNT FIGHT ABOUT NONSENSE, WHY
EVEN BOTHER, BUT IF PUSHED TO THE LIMIT
A MAN WILL DEFEND HIS HONOR.

A MAN TAKES PRIDE IN HIS APPEARANCE
ROUTINE GROOMING IS A REGULAR TASK
A MAN DOESN'T HOLD GRUDGES
A MAN DOES NOT DWELL IN THE PAST
A MAN NEVER LIES
A MAN LIVES FOR THE TRUTH
A MAN TAKES PRIDE IN BEING A MAN AND
BEING A MAN IS HIS PROOF
A MAN CAN READ "A MAN?" AND ("A MAN?") AND
SAY HEY THIS IS ABOUT ME.
IF NOT THEN A MAN IS WHO YOU SHOULD
BE TRYING TO BE
ARE YOU A MAN?

"I AM SOMEBODY"

I am somebody to somebody
even if everybody doesn't agree
I am somebody, always have been
and always will be, until this earth I leave
I am somebody to somebody
this you must believe.
Somebody said I was nobody
but does anybody agree.
I told them that I am somebody
even if that somebody is only me.
I am somebody and somebody
I will remain
I am somebody and will always
be somebody, even if,
nobody knows my name.

"WHO I AM"

I WAS A PASSENGER ON THE AMISTAD

I WAS HARRIET TUBMAN

I WAS WILLIAM STILL

I WAS NAT TURNER

I WAS FREDRICK DOUGLAS

I WAS MARY ELIZABETH BOWSER

I WAS EUNICE HUNTON CARTER

I WAS CHARLES PEARSON

I WAS MALCOLM X

I WAS MEDGAR EVERS

I WAS EMMITT TILL

I WAS ROSA PARKS

I WAS DR. MARTIN LUTHER KING JR

I WAS SEPTIMA POINSETTE CLARK

I WAS DOROTHY HEIGHT

I WAS RUBY BRIDGES

I WAS JAMES MEREDITH

I WAS NELSON MANDELA

I WAS MUHAMMED ALI

I AM COLIN KAEPERNICK...

... **N**OTICING
INJUSTICE
KNEELING
EVERYDAY

Still Being Lynched By Willie

I CAN UNDERSTAND THAT BECAUSE OF WHO I AM, YOU DON'T WANT TO HEAR ME.

I DON'T BLAME <u>YOU</u> AT ALL. IT'S BECAUSE WE ARE "STILL BEING LYNCHED BY WILLIE."

FEAR OF SPEAKING UP AND OUT AGAINST THE "ESTABLISHMENT" FOR THE SAKE OF POLITICAL CORRECTNESS.

WHAT HAPPEN'D TO "WE SHALL OVERCOME;" "I AM A MAN", ALL MEN ARE CREATED EQUAL, BEING AT THE TOP OF OUR CHECKLIST?

ON THE APPLICATION; APPLYING FOR THE STRUGGLE, WE MUST CHECK THE BOX, OTHER, BECAUSE NOWADAYS, YOU AREN'T MY SISTAH, AND HE AINT MY BROTHA

"STILL BEING LYNCHED BY WILLIE."

GAIN A LITTLE PROSPERITY AND CONFORM IS THE NORM FOR US.

WHEN WE ARE GIVEN A FEW COUPONS
WITH THE INSCRIPTION "IN GOD WE TRUST."

SPLITTING OUR BACKS NO MORE,
ITS OUR BRAINS THAT ARE BEING
WHIPPED.

STANDING ON THE AUCTION BLOCK IN
OUR MINDS, ALLOWING OUR DIGNITY TO
BE STRIPPED.

CHARACTER DECOMPOSING IS THAT PUTRID
STENCH, THAT WE CONSTANTLY SMELL BECAUSE
WE CONTINUALLY CONFORM TO WILLIE
LYNCH.

NO LONGER A NEED FOR US TO BE BARTERED,
TRADED, OR UP FOR SALE.

WE ARE ENSLAVING OURSELVES WITH DRUGS,
SEX, VIOLENCE, AND JAIL.

THE BRANCHES OF THE SYCAMORE TREE
NO LONGER BEAR THE WEIGHT.

THE NOOSE IS BEING HUNG FROM THE TREE OF OUR OWN SELF HATE.

CONTINUING TO BE THE NUMBER ONE CONTRIBUTOR TO OUR GENOCIDE SEEMS EXTREMELY SILLY.

BUT THIS IS THE CONSEQUENCE OF ALLOWING OURSELVES TO STILL BE LYNCHED BY WILLE...

`VISITORS`

JOY CALLED ME THIS MORNING
SHE SAID THAT HER, PLEASURE, AND HAPPINESS
WERE COMING TO SEE ME TODAY

IT WOULD HAVE TO BE A SHORT STAY
BECAUSE ANGER, HATE, AND HOSTILITY WERE
ON THEIR WAY

EVEN THOUGH THEY HADN'T SHOWED UP
FIRST, THEY INVITED SADNESS, GLOOM, AND
BLUE, AND BOY DO THEY REALLY KNOW HOW
TO RUIN THE MOOD.

THAT'S WHY JOY, PLEASURE, AND HAPPINESS
SAID THEY COULD ONLY STAY LONG ENOUGH TO
LIVEN UP MY DAY AND PUT A SMILE ON MY
FACE.

THEN THEY WOULD HAVE TO GO BECAUSE
IF NO ONE ELSE CAME; MISERY, DEPRESSION,
AND PAIN WOULD DEFINITELY SHOW....

B.

"Disguised"

THERE IS A DIRT ON SOME PEOPLE
THAT SOAP AND WATER CAN'T WASH AWAY.
  IT'S A FILTHY COATING
THAT SOILS WHAT THEY DO AND WHAT THEY SAY.
  NO MATTER WHO YOU ARE
OR WHAT YOU DO, THESE DIRTY PEOPLE ENJOY
TO SEE YOU STRUGGLING AND DOWN.
  AT THE SAME TIME THEY APPEAR TO CAREFORYOU
HAPPY FACES PAINTED LIKE A CLOWN.
  UNDERNEATH THE CLOWN PAINT
THEY HARBOR PURE ENVY, DECEIT, AND DISGUST.
  THE MAKEUP IS WORN IN ORDER TO GAIN YOUR
TRUST.
  ONCE YOUR TRUST IS GAINED
THEY COMMENCE TO PERFORM SURGERY ON YOURBRAIN.
  IMPLANTING THINGS YOU KNOW AREN'T TRUE
AND BEFORE YOU EVEN NOTICE, YOU DON'T LIKE YOU.
  IN ORDER TO PREVENT THIS FROM HAPPENING
YOU MUST BE SELECTIVE WITH WHOM YOU HAVE AROUND.
. DO ME A FAVOR, LOOK IN THE MIRROR
TELL ME
  IS YOUR FACE PAINTED LIKE A CLOWN?

"WAITING"

WAITING MAKES YOU WEARY
ESPECIALLY WHEN THE WAIT IS LONG
WAITING MAKES YOU TIRED
AND AT THE SAME TIME MAKES YOU
STRONG.
WAITING IS A MYSTERY
IT KEEPS YOU IN SUSPENSE
SOMETIMES ITS CLUELESS
SOMETIMES IT GIVES YOU HINTS.
WAITING BUILDS PERSEVERANCE
AND PATIENCE IN TROUBLING TIMES
WAITING SHOWS YOU THINGS
OTHERWISE NOT SEEN
ALL WILL BE SHOWN IN DUE TIME
IF YOU CHOOSE TO WAIT
BE SURE TO CHOOSE WISELY, KNOW WHAT
YOU ARE WAITING FOR AND UNDERSTAND
THAT SOMETIMES WE HAVE NO CHOICE BUT
TO WAIT
EVEN WHEN WE
DON'T WANT TO
WAIT ANYMORE.

I AM

I AM NOT MY THOUGHTS
I AM WHO RECOGNIZES MY THOUGHT
THEREFORE I AM NOT WHO I AM.

I AM. LOOKING IN FROM THE
OUTSIDE, YET I AM INSIDE AT THE SAME
TIME

I AM NOT WHO I AM, AT LEAST,
I AM NOT IN MY MIND

I AM MY THOUGHTS
ONLY I KNOW WHAT I AM THINKING

IF INDEED I AM MY THOUGHTS
HOW CAN I RECOGNIZE WHAT I AM
THINKING?

"Leaky Roof"

    The roof leaks when it rains
Losing thoughts from the strain of
my brain, trying to avoid going insane
from the constant jolts of pain
    The roof leaks when the weather
is fair, playing tricks on my mind, wind
through the cracks calling my name, but
no one is there.
    The roof leaks when it snows
needing to close the holes, they're
letting the cold in, the temperature
has dropped, and my heart has become
frozen.
    The roof leaks when the weather
is hot, now that the sun is shining,
the roof seems to be leaking in more
than one spot.
    The roof leaks and the leaking has
caused must damage, now the walls are
starting to collapse. I must find a way
to patch the leaks before my entire
house crashes to the ground, even though
I could rebuild because my foundation
is sound.

STILL I MUST REPAIR THE
LEAKS BEFORE THEY BECOME ANY WORSE.
IN ORDER TO BEGIN REPAIRS
I MUST LOCATE THE LEAKS FIRST.

B.

"Love"

I LOVE ME
DO YOU LOVE ME?
I HOPE THAT YOU DO
EVEN IF THE ANSWER IS NO
I STILL LOVE YOU
I LOVE YOU
DO YOU LOVE YOU
PLEASE SAY IT'S SO
I'M NOT SURE I WOULD UNDERSTAND
IF THE ANSWER WAS NO

"Right Now"

Close your eyes and think of the absolute worse time in your life....

Now open your eyes.

Close your eyes again and the of the most joyous time in your life

Now open your eyes

Add them both together and what do you get?

Right now!

Open your eyes

"FEAR?"

THERE'S A SHADOW FOLLOWING ME AROUND MY LIFE'S HOUSE AND I'M NOT QUITE SURE IF IT'S MY OWN.

I DESPERATELY TRY TO CATCH IT SO I CAN ASK IT TO "PLEASE LEAVE ME ALONE."

I'VE FAILED AT CATCHING IT, BUT I REMAIN HOPEFUL THAT ONE DAY I MIGHT.

WHATEVER IT IS THAT KEEPS LURKING HAS TO BE MORE THAN A SHADOW, SHADOWS CAN'T BE CAST WITH NO LIGHT.

IT IS COMPLETELY DARK IN MY HOUSE NO ILLUMINATION OR BRIGHTNESS NEAR.

COULD THE SHADOW THAT I FEEL FOLLOWING ME BE THE STALKER NAMED FEAR?

IF THAT IS THE CASE THEN FEAR AND I WILL HAVE TO MEET SOON

I'M TIRED OF LOOKING OVER MY SHOULDER IN MY OWN HOUSE, IT ISN'T BIG ENOUGH FOR THE BOTH OF US, SO FEAR, FOR YOU I DON'T HAVE ROOM.

I HOPE THAT YOU DECIDE TO STOP
SNEAKING AROUND BEHIND MY BACK.

SHOW YOUR FACE, INSTEAD OF HIDING,
COME AND TALK TO ME.

WE NEED TO COME TO AN AGREEMENT
AN UNDERSTANDING OF SOME SORT.

YOU ARENT ALLOWED IN MY LIFES HOUSE
YOU MAY COME NO FURTHER THAN THE FRONT
PORCH.

WHEN WE DO FINALLY MEET FACE TO
FACE, IT'LL HAVE TO BE THROUGH THE
SCREEN DOOR.

I CANT ALLOW YOU INSIDE MY HOUSE
YOU ARENT WELCOME HERE ANYMORE.

"Questions"

WHERE do you turn when the road you're on goes in only one direction?

HOW do you master life, is there a such thing as perfection?

WHY is it the only time you get recognition is when you've had it rough?

WHEN will someone throw in the towel and say, okay that is enough?

CAN you have a bright future, when you've had a dull past?

IS there even enough answers for all of the questions asked?

COULD it be true that some broken hearts are impossible to mend?

DO you think that it takes more energy to be enemies than it does to be friends?

WILL the lessons of life ever become any easier to understand?

DOES it make you a coward because when faced with danger you ran

WOULDN'T it make more sense to move forward instead of dwelling in the past?

YOU think there will ever be enough answers to all the questions asked?

"Lynched"

I only breathed once today
The rest of the time my breath was held.
    Afraid if I open my mouth
I may yell, scream from the pain of the
rope around my neck
    I'm being hung from the tree of
Life's rejects.
    The branch of defeat
was the branch chosen for me to be strong
    I've done nothing wrong
There was no reason for me to run.
    Now as I hang here
I wish I would have ran
I must cut myself free
But there has got to be an easier plan.
    I try to conquer one dilemma at a time
In this desperate situation of mine
But the noose around my neck keeps getting
tighter, the sun's getting brighter,
I think I may be losing consciousness
Because my body's feeling lighter.
    I've got to come up with a solution
soon, the vultures are starting to
circle

MY FEET ARE GETTING NUMB AND MY
HANDS ARE TURNING PURPLE.
            MAYBE THIS IS A BAD DREAM
AND THE TREE WILL DISAPPEAR WHEN I AWAKE
        IF NOT
I HOPE FOR A MIRACLE
                AND PRAY THAT THE
BRANCH WILL BREAK...

"DODGEBALL"

LIFE'S MISFORTUNE COMES AT YOU
FAST, LIKE A BALL IN A DODGEBALL GAME
YOU CAN EITHER
AVOID GETTING HIT OR CATCH THEM
IF YOU LET THEM HIT YOU
YOU ARE FORCED TO WATCH OTHERS GAIN
WHILE YOU SIT ON THE SIDELINE.
IF YOU CATCH THEM
ANOTHER IS THROWN AT YOU IMMEDIATELY
AFTER THE FIRST
HOW DO YOU WIN?

"NO ANSWER"

ENCOUNTERING FEELINGS OF NOT KNOWING
HOW YOU ACTUALLY FEEL. LOST HANGING ON TO
NOTHING AT ALL.

WAITING TO HIT THE BOTTOM
AFTER THIS LIFE'S LONG FREE FALL.

BOTTOM WILL NEVER BE REACHED
FREE FALLING IS NOW THE WAY FOR YOU IN
THE EMPTINESS THAT YOUR TRAPPED IN.

SIMULTANEOUSLY MIXED EMOTIONS STRIKE
THINKING YOU KNOW HOW YOU FEEL INSIDE, YET
YOU CANT EXPLAIN IT, THERE'S NO WORDS TO DESCRIBE.

ALL YOU KNOW IS YOU'RE ALIVE, BUT WHY,
WHEN ALL YOUR TIME IS SPENT FEELING WORTHLESS
SOMEONE PLEASE TELL ME THE MEANING OF THE
COMPLICATED WORD LIFE, IS THERE REALLY A
PURPOSE?

SEARCHING FOR THE ANSWER IS THE MAIN
TASK AT HAND AND IT WILL CONTROL THE MIND.

THAT IS WHY EVERYONE IS GIVEN A
DIFFERENT AMOUNT OF TIME TO FIND THE ANSWERS
TO THEMSELVES AND OPEN THE EMPTY JARS ON
THE SHELVES IN THE HALL OF CONFUSION

HOW MANY JARS DO YOU HAVE
TO OPEN BEFORE YOU COME TO THE CONCLUSION
THAT THIS IS ALL AN ILLUSION AND YOU'RE WASTING
VALUABLE TIME SEARCHING FOR THE JAR THAT
CONTAINS THE ANSWER THAT YOU'LL NEVER FIND.
THE ANSWER IS THERE BUT IT CAN'T BE
SEEN WITH THE EYES.
YOUR LIFE WILL BE SPENT ON NUMEROUS
AMOUNTS OF TRIES
UNTIL YOU FINALLY REALIZE
THERE IS NO ANSWER

Dear Heart,

I KNOW THAT IT HAS BEEN A
VERY LONG TIME SINCE WE'VE SPOKEN. I WOULD LIKE
TO APOLOGIZE FOR NOT BEING ABLE TO FILL THAT
VOID INSIDE OF YOU, THAT YOU HAVE BEEN FEELING
FOR AWHILE AND I KNOW ITS BEEN QUITE
SOME TIME SINCE I'VE MADE YOU SMILE.
HOPEFULLY IT WILL NOT BE TOO MUCH LONGER
BEFORE I AM ABLE TO MAKE THE BOND BETWEEN
US MUCH STRONGER. I KNOW THAT FOR QUITE SOME
TIME NOW YOU HAVE BEEN FEELING DESPAIR, I
HAVE BEEN FEELING IT TOO. I THOUGHT THIS ENTIRE
TIME IT WAS IN MY MIND BUT I WAS ACTUALLY
IN YOU. I'VE RECENTLY CHECKED YOUR TEMPERATURE
AND YOU NO LONGER POSSESS THAT WARMTH THAT
YOU ONCE HAD. I SHOULD HAVE RECOGNIZED IT SOONER
BUT YOUR PAIN HAS BEEN DISGUISED WITH A
LAUGH. I CANT PROMISE YOU ANYTHING BECAUSE
THERE STILL IS NO CURE FOR A BROKEN YOU. I
PROMISE YOU TO TRY MY BEST TO FIND A WAY TO
REPAIR THE BROKEN PIECES. I'VE ORDERED THE
GLUE YOU RECOMMENDED, YOU KNOW, THE "HAPPINESS
AND LOVE" BRAND. THE PROBLEM IS, ITS BACKORDERED
SO I HAD TO TAKE A RAINCHECK. AS SOON AS IT'S

AVAILABLE, ILL HAVE IT, AND I WILL
MEND YOU BACK TOGETHER AGAIN. ITS
NOT GUARANTEED THAT IT WILL HOLD
FOREVER. IM SURE THAT YOU DONT MIND
AS LONG AS IT MAKES YOU FEEL A LITTLE
BETTER. PLEASE HOLD ON TO HOPE AS
MUCH AS YOU CAN, BECAUSE I AM, AND SAVING
YOU HAS ALWAYS BEEN MY PLAN...

B

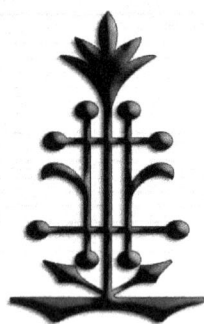

"Remote Control"

Could someone please pass the
remote control
  Life has been on pause
long enough
  Okay, now change the channel
I'm tired of the same old stuff.
  At least fast forward
So we can see what happens in the end.
  Hey, who restarted this?
  Are we at the begining again?
  Does it mean it's recording
when the light flashes red?
  I see why it was stuck on pause
This remotes batteries
        are dead.

"I vs. ME"

I CAN DO BETTER THAN ME
I JUST KNOW IT.
            HOPEFULLY ONE DAY SOON
I WILL BE GIVEN A CHANCE TO SHOW IT.
      ME, IN THE PAST
HAS MADE A LOT OF MISTAKES
      I, IS ALWAYS THE ONE
TO FORGIVE ME.
      I, GAVE ME A BREAK, ANOTHER CHANCE
AND YOU MAY AS WELL.
      I, HAS DECIDED THAT, I
WILL TRY BEING ME TODAY
      ALTHOUGH, I HAS BEEN HELD RESPONSIBLE
FOR ME MAKING ALL OF THOSE PAST MISTAKES
      I, HAS DECIDED TO GIVE ME A BREAK.
      I, WOULD BE WRONG TO GIVE
UP ON ME.
      I, IS ALL THAT ME HAS, BESIDES
I IS THE ONLY ONE THAT HAS LOOKED
OUT FOR ME IN THE PAST.
      I, SHOULDN'T BE SO QUICK TO
GIVE UP ON ME SO FAST.
      I, HAS DECIDED TO GIVE ME
ANOTHER CHANCE.

I, HAS MADE UP ITS MIND
I, HAS DECIDED TO GIVE ME
ANOTHER CHANCE
            AND SO SHOULD YOU...

"Love a Child"

Be sure that you do
how could you not love a child.
    Dont they always seem to cheer
you up when they cast that innocent
smile.
    How about the questions they ask
depending on your honest answer
because before they asked they really
diont know.
    Or what about their non-judgemental
love, that they arent afraid to show.
    One day they will be you because
you were once them.
    All the knowledge that you've gained
you pass to them to store within.
    Love a child, how could you not,
when you do, you'll never want to stop.
    The love that you give will be
appreciated when they grow and
reach the top.
    Love a child unconditionally
they all grow up and lose that title.

ALL YOU'LL HAVE LEFT
IS MEMORIES OF THEIR GAMES, PLAYS,
AND RECITLES.
    LOVE A CHILD YOU MUST
HOW COULD YOU NOT?
    BESIDES YOU NEVER KNOW
THE LOVE YOU GIVE
        MAY BE ALL OF THE LOVE
            THAT THEY'VE GOT.

Ⓑ.

"PREY"

LIKE ENTERING A TRAIN OR CROWDED BUS
CLUTCHING ALL THAT YOU OWN, YOU DON'T KNOW
WHO TO TRUST.

You KNOW THAT YOU'RE BEING PRAYED UPON,
YOU CAN FEEL THE PREDATOR NEAR.

You CAN'T PLACE EXACTLY WHO IT IS
SO EVERYONE YOU FEAR

CONSTANTLY WATCHING YOUR BACK
FROM BEHIND PEOPLE LOVE TO CREEP

You NEVER ALLOW YOUR DEFENSES DOWN,
SO ONE EYE IS OPEN WHILE ASLEEP.

YOU'RE NOT SURE OF WHERE YOU ARE
ALL YOU KNOW IS IT'S NOT HOME

NOT SURE OF WHO OR WHAT TO FEAR
BUT YOU DEFINITELY FEAR THE UNKNOWN.

You TRY TO PLAY IT COOL
WHICH IS BECOMING HARDER WITH TIME.

NOW SURE OF WHAT'S ACTUALLY HAPPENING
ARE YOU OVERREACTING, OR IS IT ALL IN
YOUR MIND.

JUST TO BE ON THE SAFE SIDE
YOU KEEP UP YOUR GUARD, THAT'S THE ONLY
WAY TO AVOID YOUR HEART BEING SCARRED.

BUT WHAT IF YOU'RE WRONG
THINK ABOUT THE GOOD PEOPLE YOU PUSHED
AWAY.

     I GUESS THAT'S THE CHANCE THAT
YOU'LL HAVE TO TAKE. TO AVOID
     BEING PREYED
      UPON TODAY

Untitled

Pain is life, joy is hurt, loneliness is true and carrying it hurts.

Love is confusing, truth is a lie, excuses are evident when tears are dry.

Making it work is tiresome, giving up is in doubt, picking up the pieces is dangerous and difficult to figure out.

Wrong is normal, right has been left, pain is miserable, and fear is death....

"You"

You are the only you
so don't be afraid of being yourself.

    You were individually given your own
personality, mind, body, soul, and health.

    Stop being afraid of being singled out
that you go to great extremes
to copy others actions, lifestyles, looks,
and dreams.

    And for what?! Just to fit in?!

    Life is a game given to <u>you</u>
so <u>you</u> must play to win

    Life was given to <u>You</u>, so by <u>you</u>,
it has to be led.

    It was not intended for you to
try to simulate something that you
saw, heard, or read.

    Life doesn't require you to be a certain
height, age, color, or weight

    Life doesn't mind if you start living
it late.

    Just as long as you do and its
true, that you are living it for
you

LIFE'S SATISFACTION CAN AND WILL
BE GUARANTEED
WHEN YOU SUCCEED
AT PROVING TO YOURSELF
THAT BEING YOU IS ALL
THAT YOU NEED.

Untitled

My love is a choice, not a feeling.

Feelings change, but my love for you stays the same.

God made the choice of whom I should love.

He blessed me, by choosing my life to place you in.

He chose you, he chose me, he chose us, and so do I.

Ⓑ.

"WITHOUT MY HEART"

THOUGHTS OF YOUR SEXY WAYS KEEP ME
SMILING, DAZED, AND IN A ZONE.
THE SOUND OF YOUR VOICE IS SO SWEET
I SWEAR I TASTE YOUR WORDS WHEN I'M ALONE
IMAGES OF YOUR BEAUTY
I'M FORCED TO KEEP THEM NEAR
YOU NEVER RETURNING TO ME
HAS BECOME MY BIGGEST FEAR.
I MISS YOU PROFUSELY
YOUR TANTALIZING SCENT STILL LINGERS IN
MY AIR
WISHING I COULD HOLD YOU CLOSE
AND RUN MY FINGERS THROUGH YOUR HAIR.
"JUST-TO-BE-CLOSE-TO-YOU-GIRRRRLLL"
JUST LIKE THAT OLD SONG.
TRYING TO FIGURE OUT EVERYDAY
WHEN, WHERE, AND HOW DID I GO WRONG.
WONDERING DO YOU THINK OF ME AS I
THINK OF YOU, AND IF SO, TO EASE THE AGONY
EXACTLY WHAT DO YO DO?
DOES YOUR HEART ACHE LIKE MINE?
AM I EVEN ON YOUR MIND?
OR AM I JUST WASTING MY TIME?

I PROBABLY WILL NEVER
UNDERSTAND, OR EVER KNOW, BUT I REFUSE
TO ACCEPT DEFEAT.

IF YOU FEEL THE SAME WAY I DO
THEN MAYBE ONE DAY OUR SOULS WILL AGAIN
MEET.

UNTIL THAT DAY COMES
IM FORCED TO CONTINUE REMINISCING.
WITHOUT YOU IN MY LIFE
        I CANT LIVE
            BECAUSE MY HEART
                REMAINS MISSING.

"You Choose"

THERE IS A TIME FOR LOVE
AND A TIME FOR HATE.
A TIME TO MOVE
AND A TIME TO WAIT.
THERE IS A TIME FOR SADNESS
AND A TIME FOR TEARS.
A TIME TO BE BRAVE
AND A TIME FOR FEAR
THERE IS A TIME TO BE WRONG
AND A TIME TO BE RIGHT
A TIME TO GIVE UP
AND A TIME TO FIGHT
IF YOU HAVE A SECOND TO HATE
YOU HAVE A MINUTE TO LOVE
WHICH CAN TURN INTO HOURS
IF YOU NEVER GIVE UP.

YOU CHOOSE!

WISHING

     I WISH I WERE A TREE
A TREE DOESN'T HAVE TO WORRY ABOUT
WHEN IT GROWS UP WHAT IT WANTS TO BE
IN LIFE.
     I WISH I WERE A FLOWER
A FLOWER NEVER WORRIES IF IT WILL EVER
FIND A WIFE
     I WISH I WERE A BIRD
THE FREE'EST OF THEM ALL
SOARING THROUGH THE SKY NEVER
FEARING IT WILL FALL
     I WISH.

"Cage Fight"

Cagefighting has become a sport
well its my everyday life.

Forced to fight, placed in a submission
hold, that out of I must find a way.

As the choke hold becomes tighter,
the thought of tapping out does arise.

I refuse to accept defeat
even though the pain is starting to
show in my eyes.

In this cage fighting myself
make any wrong moves and I only
end up hurt.

I wasnt trained for this type of fighting
Im being attacked from the inside
first.

No matter what techniques are used,
I must not lose, the only match of my
career.

This is the one and only chance
I have, I must endure my fear.

As I try to pry my why out of
harm's grasp, Im starting to become
enraged.

I harness the rage and

TURN IT INTO POWER
TO HELP ME FIGHT MY WAY OUT OF
THIS CAGE. B.

"NOW"

IF YOU HAVE A RECOLLECTION ABOUT
SOMETHING, YOU DO IT AT THAT VERY MOMENT

IF YOU LOOK FOWARD TO SOMETHING
YOU DO IT AT THAT VERY MOMENT.

THAT VERY MOMENT IS ACTUALLY
THE ONLY TIME THAT EXISTS.

NOW OR THE PRESENT IS
ALL THERE REALLY IS.

FUTURE AND PAST
ARE ALL IN THE MIND.

WHICH LEAVES US WITH
ONLY ONE TYPE OF TIME...

... NOW! Ⓑ.

"FALLEN"

THROUGHOUT THE LONELY DAYS
DURING THE GLOOMY NIGHTS.
I PICTURE YOUR BEAUTIFUL SMILE
REASSURING ME THAT EVERYTHING WILL BE
ALRIGHT
THOUGHTS OF YOU IN MY ARMS
ALL I CAN DO IS WISH THAT YOUR HEART
COULD BEAT NEXT TO MINE AND I COULD
FEEL YOUR GENTLE KISS.
THESE FEELINGS THAT I HAVE FOR
YOU ARE A BLESSING FROM THE MAN UP
ABOVE.
EVERY NIGHT I PRAY THAT HE
CATCHES ME
BECAUSE I'VE FALLEN
IN LOVE.

"Imagine"

Close your eyes for a moment
Imagine that you are me.
    Treated like a hostage, captured
and taken somewhere that you don't
want to be.
    There's a putrid odor in the air
Its the smell of my lost soul decomposing
    The halls that you are exploring
are very dark and every door that you go
through, behind you they are closing.
    You are being followed by hate
disguised as a friend.
    Every turn that you make
wanting to help it pretends.
    Here in this cellar
everyone has been cursed or damned.
    Smiling hurts the face
and it is forbidden to laugh.
    There's a clock on the wall
Can you see it, its without an hour,
It only has a second hand, because
thats all the time that it takes to
realize coming here was not part of
the plan.

CAN YOU FEEL THE COLD, CLAMMY, SWEAT THAT COVERS YOUR BODY AS YOU VENTURE ON.

THERE IS A ROOM I WOULD LIKE FOR YOU TO ENTER, YOU ARE ALMOST THERE IT WONT BE LONG.

THIS ROOM HOLDS MY HEART THERE IS SOMETHING ON IT I WOULD LIKE FOR YOU TO SEE.

JUST A LITTLE BIT FURTHER KEEP YOUR EYES CLOSED FOR ME.

NOW YOU HAVE ARRIVED, ITS ALRIGHT, YOU MAY OPEN YOUR EYES.

I WANT YOU TO TELL ME CAN YOU SEE HOW BADLY MY HEART HAS BEEN SCARRED.

IT DOESNT BEAT LIKE IT SHOULD AND ITS SURFACE IS HARD.

MY REASON FOR BRINGING YOU HERE IS BECAUSE I HOPED THAT YOU COULD MEND IT.

I THOUGHT IT WOULD MEND ITSELF IF ONLY I PRETENDED THAT NOTHING WAS AWRY.

MY EMOTIONS ARE STORED IN A
SEPARATE ROOM, THEREFORE I AM
UNABLE TO CRY.
SO I'M ASKING YOU
WHAT DO I DO?
I WAS HOPING THAT YOU COULD
HELP, IF YOU CLOSED YOUR EYES AND
TRIED TO SEE, EXACTLY HOW IT WOULD
FEEL IF YOU WERE ME...

℟

"PRAY"

HAVE YOU PRAYED TODAY?
    IF NOT THEN YOU PROBABLY SHOULD
IF YOU KNEW THE OUTCOME, I'M SURE THAT
YOU PROBABLY WOULD
    THE OUTCOME IS NOT UP TO US
EVEN THE MOST DESTRUCTIVE THING ON EARTH
BEARS THE WORDS "IN GOD WE TRUST."
    THAT SHOULD TELL YOU SOMETHING
OR AT LEAST LET YOU KNOW GOD IS
REAL
        GIVE IT A TRY
        PRAY TODAY
AND TOMORROW LET ME KNOW
        HOW YOU
            FEEL (B).

"ALPHABET"

AFTER
BEING
CONFINED
DETERMINATION
EKING
FAILURE
GOD
HAS
INEVITABLY
JUSTIFIED
KNOWINGLY
LIMITING
MY
NOSTALGIA
OUSTING
PREVIOUSLY
QUESTIONED
RESISTANCE
SOMETIMES
TOWARDS
UNDERSTANDING
VARIOUS
WICKED
XENOPHOBIC
YEARS
ZIGZAGGING
THROUGH MY MIND . . . .

"DREAMS"

I DREAM WHEN I'M ASLEEP
AS WELL AS WHEN I'M AWAKE
   I TRY TO DECIPHER WHAT DREAMS
ARE REAL AND WHICH ONES ARE FAKE
   PATIENTLY AWAITING MY DREAMS TO
COME TRUE, THEY WILL ONE DAY I JUST KNOW IT
WHEN GIVEN THE CHANCE I HOPE I DON'T
BLOW IT.
   ALL MY DREAMS SEEM GOOD
AT LEAST WHILE THEY LAST.
   SOME FADE AWAY, BUT WILL RETURN,
IN MY MEMORY THEY STAY STASHED.
   MY DREAMS ARE A HIEROGLYPHIC
WRITTEN ON THE WALLS OF MY BRAIN,
GIVING ME DIRECTION
   SHOWING BOTH PAST AND PRESENT,
OFFERING ME PROTECTION, REMEMBERING
EVENT THROUGH OUT THE DAY, BUT WHEN
I EXPERIENCED THEM I WAS NAPPING.
   MY DREAMS CONTAIN PLACES I'VE NEVER
BEEN AND PEOPLE I'VE NEVER MET BEFORE
   HOW IS THAT EVEN POSSIBLE FOR MY BRAIN
TO STORE.
   MY DREAMS ARE CONTINUOUS

DREAMWORLD AND REALITY HAVE TOGETHER
BEEN SPLICED.
          WHAT APPEARS IN A DREAM
WILL EVENTUALLY RE-APPEAR IN MY CONSCIOUS LIFE.
          NOW I'VE COME TO THIS CONCLUSION
I MUST DREAM WHAT I TRULY FEEL
          DAY AFTER DAY ITS BECOMING HARDER
TO DECIDE WHICH DREAMS ARE FAKE
          AND WHICH ONES ARE
          REAL...

"LIFE THE SHOW"

THERE ARE NO AUDITIONS
YOU ARE AUTOMATICALLY GIVEN A PART
GRANTED ONE SINGLE TRY, NO PRACTICE
RUN OR REHEARSALS.

BEFORE YOU REALIZE IT THE SHOW
HAS ALREADY BEGUN AND THERE ARE NO
COMMERCIALS.

THERE ARE NO RETAKES, YOU HAVE TO
WORK THROUGH YOUR MISTAKES. EVEN THOUGH
ONCE IN AWHILE YOU WILL BE GIVEN A BREAK.

THERE IS NO SCRIPT, MOST OF THE LIVE
AUDIENCE WOULD LOVE TO SEE YOU FAIL. WHICH
IS REAL EASY TO DO BECAUSE THERE IS NO
DIRECTOR TO YELL

CUT!

LET'S TAKE IT FROM THE TOP.
THERE ARENT ANY STUNT DOUBLES, MAKEUP
ARTIST, OR PROPS.

ALTHOUGH IT IS A SITCOM, ONE DAY ITS
SEASON WILL HAVE TO END. WHEN IT FINALLY
DOES, ITS EPISODES CAN NEVER BE VIEWED
AGAIN

FOR YOUR PERFORMANCE, YOU WILL NOT
WIN A GOLDEN GLOBE, OSCAR, OR RECEIVE A
STAR ON THE WALK OF FAME.

You will be hurt during filming, sometimes with nothing to ease the pain.

Before acting out your part to avoid mistakes you must think twice.

Whats the name of this show you ask?

Its the #1 show and I think its called LIFE.

"Reflections"

Looking at myself in the mirror
I start to stare deeply.
   The only time I am who I am
Is in a dream when I am asleep.
   Then I awaken
And the mirror's reflection of me is
Unable to bear.
   I see myself staring back
But still I am not all there.
   Then the mirror shatters into a
Thousand pieces but is not broken
   I've been given the key
To unlock the doors to my life but it
Still will not open.
   As I pick up the pieces of the mirror
That did not break
   I ask myself, how much more of
This can I take?
   I continue to look in at the
Reflection in the mirror, thinking
What could be worse?
   I guess my life has become like a
Butterfly that wasn't a caterpillar
First . . . Ⓡ

"VERB'S LOVE"

LOVE DID,

      LOVE DOES,

            LOVE WILL,

LOVE SHOULD,

      LOVE SHALL,

           LOVE COULD,

LOVE WOULD,

      LOVE CAN,

         LOVE IS!

Concluding Thoughts

"Don't Build A House
Where You
Should Only Pitch
A Tent"

www.RIVObooks.com

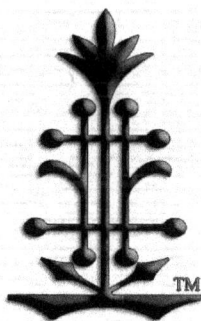

www.RIVObooks.com

www.ingramcontent.com/pod-product-compliance
Lightning Source LLC
Chambersburg PA
CBHW061742020426
42331CB00006B/1332